Green Planet

Christine Lindop

Christine Lindop was born in New Zealand, and taught English in France and Spain before settling in Great Britain. She has written and adapted more than twenty books, including *Australia and New Zealand* in the Oxford Bookworms series, and *The Turn of the Screw* in the Dominoes series. In her free time she likes reading, watching films, and cooking. Her favourite part of this planet is her vegetable and fruit garden, which is 'as big as a swimming pool, and just as much fun'.

Great Clarendon Street, Oxford, OX2 6DP,
United Kingdom

Oxford University Press is a department of the University of Oxford. It furthers the University's objective of excellence in research, scholarship, and education by publishing worldwide. Oxford is a registered trade mark of Oxford University Press in the UK and in certain other countries

First edition published in Dominoes in 2004

2026 2025 2024
10 9 8 7 6 5

ISBN: 978 0 19 460848 0 Book
ISBN: 978 0 19 460847 3 Book and Audio Pack

Audio not available separately

Printed in China

This book is printed on paper from certified and well-managed sources.

ACKNOWLEDGEMENTS

Cover image: Getty (aerial view of river, Point Reyes National Seashore, California, United States/Artur Debat/Moment RF).

Illustrations by: Martin Sanders/Beehive Illustration pp.15, 59.

The publisher would like to thank the following for their permission to reproduce photographs: Alamy pp.1 (Sentinel-1 satellite in orbit/Science History Images), 4 (Fossil of extinct Pleistocene mammal, Channel islands, California/Kevin Schafer), 5 (Origin of Species by Charles Darwin/Derek Croucher), (title page of Origin of Species by Charles Darwin/Paul Carstairs), 8 (volunteers planting tree/PG Arphexad), 10 (World Wildlife Fund (WWF) activists demonstrate on the sidelines of the UN Climate Change Conference COp.16 in Cancun December 5, 2010/Reuters), 17 (A view of a street flooded with sea water at Mayangan village in Subang, Indonesia's West Java province July 16, 2010/Reuters), 23 (Golden Toad (Bufo periglenes) males, breeding aggregation, extinct, Monteverde Cloud Forest Reserve, Costa Rica/Minden Pictures), 36 (whale watchers and humpback whale (Megaptera novaeangliae)/blickwinkel), 52 (CoppenHill Power Plant, Copenhagen, Denmark – distant view with clouds and green roof slope/Architect: BIG Bjarke Ingels Group, 2019/Hufton+Crow-VIEW), 55 (Wikkelhouse/Marcus Brandt/dpa), 58 (Turtle eating a plastic cup drifting in the middle of a huge garbage patch floating in the ocean/Pally), 59 (A black footed albatross chick with plastics in its stomach lies dead on Midway Atoll in the Northwestern Hawaiian Islands/H.S. Photos); Getty ppiii (scenic view of lake by trees against sky, Yosemite National Park/ Greg Clay/500px), 2 (Iceberg A-74, Brunt Ice Shelf, Antarctica, 14 March 2021/Gallo Images/Orbital Horizon/Copernicus Sentinel Data 2021), (Satellite view of wildfires in Southern Turkey, 29 July 2021/Gallo Images/ Orbital Horizon/Copernicus Sentinel Data 2021), (Mediterranean hurricane (Medicane) Ianos makes landfall in Greece, 17 September 2020/ Gallo Images/Orbital Horizon/Copernicus Sentinel Data 2020), 3 (1890 – Illustration of the H.M.S. Beagle carrying Charles Darwin's expedition in the Straits of Magellan, Mt. Sarmiento in the distance/Bettmann), (Portrait of a young Charles Darwin in 1840; watercolor and chalk on paper by George Richmond, 1840/GraphicaArtis/Getty Images), 4, 6 (Four or the species of finch observed by Darwin on the Galapagos Islands/Hulton Archive/Print Collector), 8 (spraying pesticides/Sandro Balbuena/EyeEm), (Rachel Carson/JHU Sheridan Libraries/Gado), 14 (Al Gore attends a press conference for An Inconvenient Sequel: Truth to Power/Matthias Nareyek/ Getty Images for Paramount Pictures), 17 (Sumarti, looks out at the small garden in front of her house in an abandoned factory filled with standing water in which there is a small community living November 24, 2015 in Jakarta, Indonesia/Ed Wray/Getty Images AsiaPac), 26 (The Buffalo Hunt by Paul Kane/Francis G. Mayer/Corbis/VCG via Getty Images), 27 (John Muir (1838-1914) Scottish-born American naturalist, engineer, writer and pioneer of conservation/Universal Images Group Editorial), 28 (Alan Rabinowitz, the CEO of Panthera/Nurphoto), 30 (scenic view of lake by trees against sky, Yosemite National Park/Greg Clay/500px), (minke whale/Kerstin Meyer/Moment), 34 (penguin trapped in plastic/ tsvibrav/iStock), 37 (Crew members of the marine conservation organisation Sea Shepherd Conservation Society (SSCS) aboard a speed boat navigate towards the Sam Simon ship/Loic Venanc/AFP), 39 (satellite view of the Fukushima Dai-ichi Nuclear Power plant after a massive earthquake and subsequent tsunami on March 14, 2011 in Futaba, Japan/DigitalGlobe), 40 (Fire boats battle a fire at the off shore oil rig Deepwater Horizon April 21, 2010 in the Gulf of Mexico/U.S. Coast Guard), 41 (A brown pelican coated in heavy oil wallows in the surf June 4, 2010 on East Grand Terre Island, Louisiana/Win McNamee), (a brown pelican (Pelecanus occidentalis) is washed at the International Bird Rescue Research Center in Fort Jackson, Louisiana/ Daniel Beltra/Greenpeace/Tribune News Service), 42 (Chernobyl nuclear power plant a few weeks after the disaster. Chernobyl, Ukraine, USSR, May 1986/Igor Kostin/Laski Diffusion), (Chernobyl's Safe Confinement covering the 4th block of Chernobyl Nuclear power plant/Sergei Supinsky/AFP), 43 (a house is dismantled while bags containing radioactive substances piled up at the "difficult-to-return zone" on the 9th anniversary of the Great East Japan Earthquake on March 11, 2020 in Futaba, Fukushima, Japan/The Asahi Shimbun via Getty Images), (a rescue worker walks around houses ruined by a tsunami after an 8.9 magnitude earthquake on March 12, 2011 in Minamisoma, Fukushima, Japan/Sankei), 44 (a coal mining operation in West Virginia where operators have blasted off a mountaintop to uncover valuable, low-sulphur coal seams/Pete Souza/Chicago Tribune/Tribune News Service), 48 (couple riding electric bicycles at Old Warehouse District, Hamburg/Westend61), 50 (Greta Thunberg gesturesduring a Fridays for Future students' strike on October 1, 2021 on the sidelines of the Youth4Climate and Pre-COp.26 events in Milan/Miguel Medina/AFP), 51 (Numerous cyclists on a city street in the afternoon, Copenhagen, Denmark/Pel_1971/iStock Editorial), 52 (A youth has fun at Amager Bakke, aka Copenhill, an artificial ski slope and recreational hiking area on top of a resource handling centre in Copenhagen/Mads Claus Rasmussen/Ritzau Scanpix/AFP), 53 (mountain valley at sunrise/Biletskiy_Evgeniy), 54 (lab/Morsa Images/Digital Vision), (bacteria/iStockphoto), 55 (AeroFarms/Angela Weiss/AFP), 58 (Sailing in the Stockholm archipelago/Photomick/E+), 59 (Charles Moore poses aboard his research catamaran/Jonathan Alcorn/Bloomberg), (Charles Moore holds an ocean water sample with debris from the 'Great Pacific Garbage Patch'/Jonathan Alcorn/ Bloomberg), 61 ((Fire boats battle a fire at the off shore oil rig Deepwater Horizon April 21, 2010 in the Gulf of Mexico/U.S. Coast Guard), 64 (two species of finch observed by Darwin on the Galapagos Islands/Hulton Archive/Print Collector); Greenpeace p.11 (The Phyllis Cormack at sea, at the Mendocino seamounts/Rex Weyler), (Greenpeace logo/Sylvain HENRI), (Greenpeace action against Norwegian whaling ship Kato, North Sea/John Cunningham); Oxford University Press ppiv (plastic bottles) (fossil/Phaitoon Sutunyawatchai/ Shutterstock), (Earth from space/MarcelClemens/Shutterstock), (earthquake damage/photo story/Shutterstock), (glacier/Volodymyr Goinyk/Shutterstock), 4 (elephant), 11 (whale), 20 ('Sparkle' spray bottle), 46 (fossil); Shutterstock ppiv (mountain and meadows with horses in the summer pasture/ABCDstock), (flooded road in Jiujiang, China, 2017/humphery), (forest/dugdax), 2 (the Indonesian volcano Anak Krakatau – volcanic ash and steam streaming southwest over the waters of the Sunda Strait, on September 22, 2018/ESA/UPI), 7 (Close up shot on a metallic blue cuckoo wasp/Chui Wui Jing), (scientist with test tube/Alexander Raths), (A spring landscape on the hills/bdavid32), (hand planting pumpkin seeds in fresh dark soil/ FotoDuets), (toucan bird/R.M. Nunes), (gas giant/Vadim Sadovski) 12 (the tropical rainforest of the Taman Negara National Park. Kuala Tahan, Pahang State, Malaysia/travelwild), 13 (A Tornado forming in the evening from a supercell/solarseven), 15 (coal/zhengchengbao), 16 (snow geese/Delmas Lehman), 18 (fresh green leaf highlighted by the sun/tabaca), 18 (rainforest/Sorn340 Studio Images), 20 (rainforest layers illustration/BlueRingMedia),(capuchin monkey cub on tree branch/LeonP), (black viper snake on tree/halimqd), (toucan/Oleksiy Mark), (Red parrot (Macaw parrot)/Petr Salinger), (Sri Lankan leopard (Panthera pardus kotiya) resting on fallen tree over stream in rain forest, native to Sri Lanka/Philippe Clement), (Pills in medicine bottle/ piotr_pabijan), (banana/Shironagasukujira), (coffee/SharkPaeCNX), (coconuts/Inna Dodor), (dark chocolate/Gulsina), (Brazil nuts/nada54), (Bottle of shampoo/Konstantin Faraktinov), 22 (Deforestation/Rich Carey), (palm tree plantation/apiguide), 24 (Boa constrictor/Sanne Romijn Fotografie), 25 (bison/Ghost Bear), (jaguar/Mikadun), (Yellowstone national park sign/blvdone), 26 (bison/O.S. Fisher), 28 ((jaguar/Anan Kaewkhammul), 29 (jaguar/milosk50), (healthy coral reef/Tunatura/iStockphoto), (bleached coral reef/Brett Monroe Garner/ Moment RF), 31 (Emperor Penguin on the frozen Weddell Sea/Roger Clark ARPS BPE1), (Polar bear on the pack ice/Alexey Seafarer), 32 (Emperor Penguins/vladsilver), 33 (Adelie Penguin (pygoscelis adeliae) group Leaping into Ocean, Paulet Island in Antarctica/ slowmotiongli), (King Penguin swimming/The Image Bank RF/Kevin Schafer), 34 (Antarctic krill (Euphausia superba)/Auscape International Pty Ltd), 35 (Young Polar bear (Ursus maritimus) foraging for food in the dump, Churchill, Manitoba, Canada/ Splashdown/Michael Nolan), (seal pup/Eric Isselee), 45 (Wind turbines/ space-kraft), (solar panels/Digital Media Pro), 48 ((filling water bottle/ Stefaniya Gutovska), 50 (Greta Thunberg holds a placard reading 'School strike for the climate', during a protest against climate change outside the Swedish parliament in Stockholm, 30 November 2018/Hanna Franzen/EPA-EFE), 52 (skiing/gorillaimages), 53 (group of scientists working at the laboratory/Alexander Raths), 54 (footprints/ Naypong Studio), (cycle lane/Dmitry Naumo), (ski/IM_photo), (fuel/ Seasontime), 56 (Animal crossing bridge on Trans Canada Highway – Banff National Park/Yaya Ernst), (Black bear with two cubs crossing the road in Canadian Rockies, Banff National Park/Marina Poushkina), 57 (Rare Blue Iguana, also known as Grand Cayman Iguana (Cyclura lewisi/Frontpage), 59 (plastic bottles/Take Photo), 62 (rainforest with mountains beyond/Sorn340 Studio Images), 63 (Emperor Penguins/ vladsilver), 67 (snow geese/Delmas Lehman).

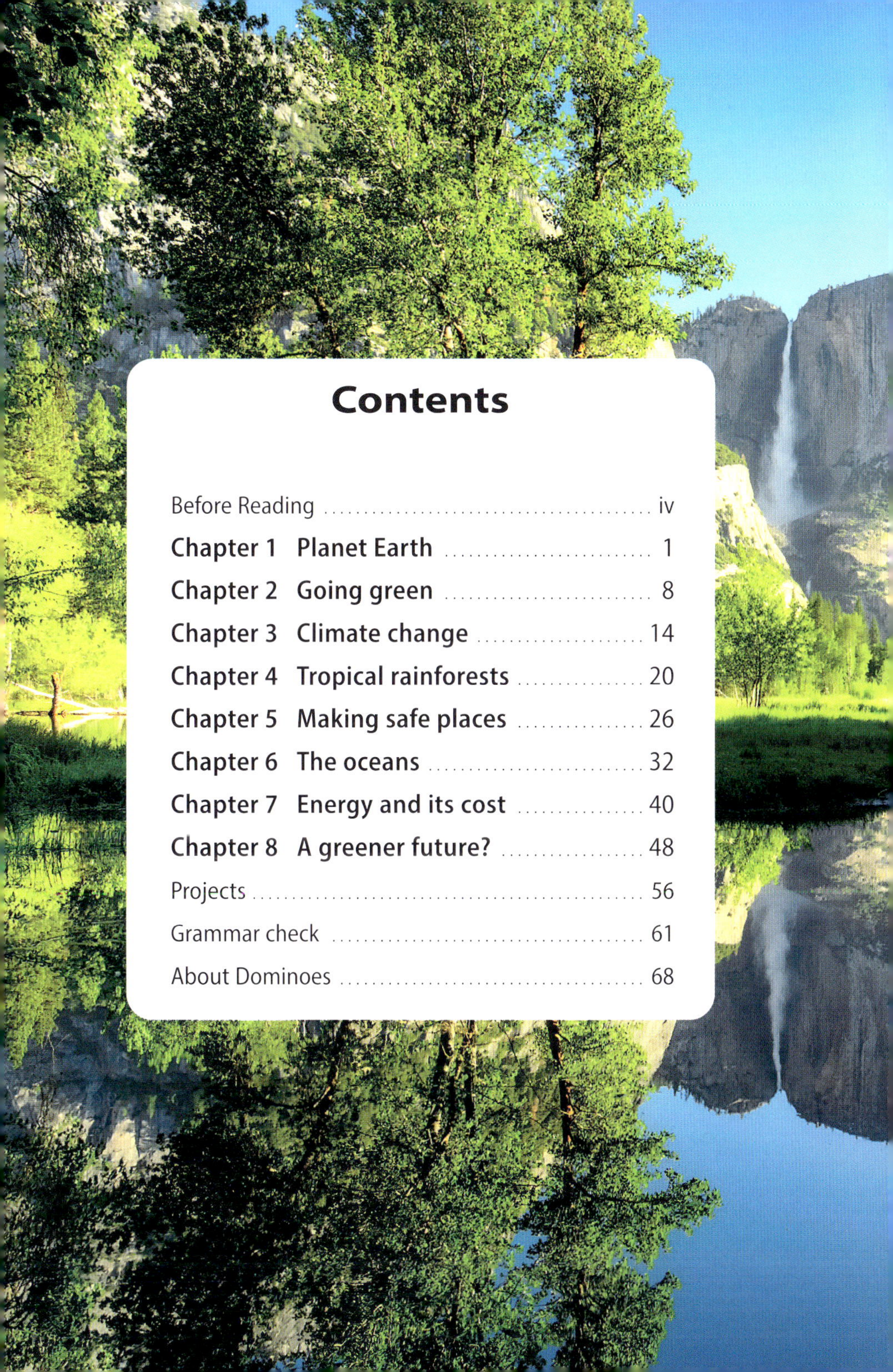

Contents

BEFORE READING

1 Match the pictures with the dictionary definitions below.

- **a** ☐ **Earth** the world; we live on the Earth
- **b** ☐ **earthquake** when the ground suddenly shakes and moves
- **c** ☐ **forest** a lot of trees which are together in one place
- **d** ☐ **fossil** something that lived long ago which is now hard and in the ground or in a stone
- **e** ☐ **flood** when there is too much water
- **f** ☐ **ice** water that is very cold and hard
- **g** ☐ **plastic** we use plastic to make lots of different things, like water bottles
- **h** ☐ **environment** everything around us: the ground, the air, rivers and seas, animals, trees, and other plants

2 Here are two groups that want to help the environment. Find out the answers to the questions for each group.

Greenpeace	World Wide Fund for Nature (WWF)

- **a** When and where did they start their work?
- **b** What did they try to do at first?
- **c** What are they trying to do today?

1. Planet Earth

Look up into the night sky. You can't see it, but somewhere up there is *Sentinel-1*, two **satellites** that work together. *Sentinel-1* travels 700 kilometres above the Earth and goes round the Earth once every 100 minutes. It takes pictures of all of the Earth and sends them back to **scientists** here every six days. *Sentinel-1* began doing this in April 2014, and since then, it has worked twenty-four hours per day. It can take pictures by day and by night, and through clouds and storms. And *Sentinel-1* isn't alone. *Sentinels 2, 3, 4,* and 5 are all at work up there, too.

There's a lot of **information** about our **planet** in *Sentinel-1's* pictures. Scientists can use this information in different ways. When the terrible storm Idai hit Malawi, Mozambique, and Zimbabwe in 2019, scientists got information from *Sentinel-1* about the floods that followed. Workers there used this information to get help to people who needed it.

In 2016, there were two bad earthquakes in Italy. Hundreds of people died, and thousands lost their homes. Scientists are now **studying** the pictures from *Sentinel-1*, looking for very small **changes** in the **land** in Italy. This can help them to know about earthquakes that are coming, and to make plans to help people.

satellite something that travels around the Earth to get information and take pictures

scientist a person who studies the world

information facts and numbers

planet the Earth is a planet

study to learn about something

change to become different or not the same

land the part of the Earth that is not the sea; you can walk on land

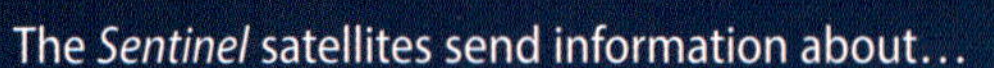

The *Sentinel* satellites send information about…

- changes in the ice in the Arctic and Antarctic, and where ice is moving in the sea
- early news of floods and storms
- early news of big wild fires
- early news of earthquakes
- early news of changes in volcanoes
- information about the sea – for example, how much food there is for fish

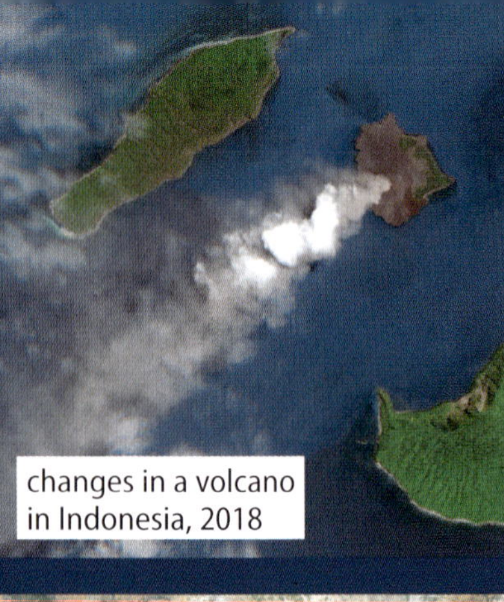

changes in a volcano in Indonesia, 2018

moving ice in Antarctica, 2021

wild fires in Turkey, 2021

a hurricane in Athens, Greece, 2020

Charles Darwin and the finches

One hundred and eighty-three years before *Sentinel-1* left the Earth to work above us, another journey began – a journey that changed the way that people think about life on Earth. On 27 December 1831, a ship called *HMS Beagle* left England on a five-year journey to South America and the Pacific. On the *Beagle*, there was a clever young man called Charles Darwin. He was very interested in **plants** and animals, so when scientists asked him to travel with them, he said yes. He didn't get any money for his work on the ship, but this didn't matter to Darwin. He was just excited to learn about the plants and animals in all these new places.

Charles Darwin

Born: 1809 in England

Died: 1887 in England

Facts: At first, Darwin studied to be a doctor; then he studied to work for the church. He is most famous for his work studying plants and animals.

plant a small living green thing with leaves and sometimes with flowers

fact something that's true

seed when you put this in the ground a plant grows from it

beak a bird's body part; it's hard, and it's used for eating

insect a very small animal with six legs

idea something that you think

species a group of animals or plants that are the same

In South America and in the Galapagos Islands, Darwin looked at some small birds called finches. He saw that the finches were not all the same. Finches that ate big **seeds** had short, strong **beaks**, while finches that ate **insects** had long, narrow beaks. 'Perhaps these birds were once the same but because they lived in different places and ate different food, they slowly changed,' Darwin thought.

Finches from the Galapagos Islands, 1835

This was a new **idea** at the time. Until then, most scientists thought that animal and plant **species** didn't change. So how did they explain fossils that were different from living species? Scientists thought that from time to time something happened on the Earth which killed all of one species, and then a new species took its place. But when Darwin saw these different finches, he began to think that perhaps this wasn't true.

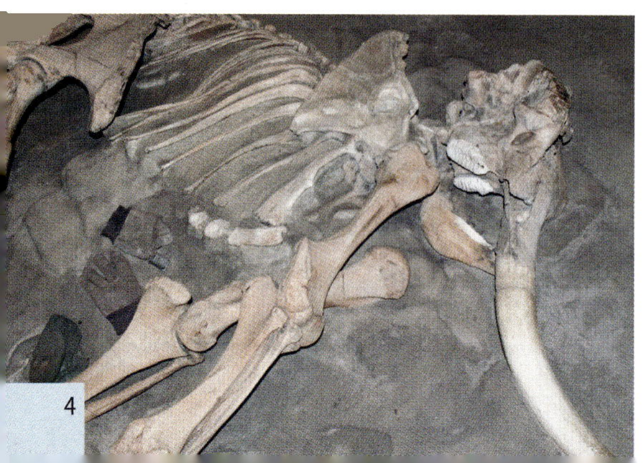

After Darwin came back from his travels, he spent a long time studying, reading, and writing about his ideas. In 1859, Darwin's book *On the Origin of Species* arrived in bookshops. All 1,250 books were sold on the first day. In this book, Darwin said that any species could change over time into a new species. He also said that when something changes in a place – for example, when the weather changes, or when there isn't much food – animal and plant species can live through these difficult times by changing slowly. Many people were interested in the ideas in Darwin's book. Some people agreed with them, but some got very angry about them.

These days, we know that Darwin's ideas were right: plant and animal species do change very slowly over time. We also know that our environment is always changing because of the things that people do, and because of storms, floods, or earthquakes. Information from satellites, like the *Sentinel* satellites, can help us to see the changes that are happening on the Earth. Sometimes these changes happen quickly, sometimes slowly, sometimes in good ways, and sometimes in bad ways.

Over the last fifty years, more and more people have begun to ask questions about dangerous changes in the environment. How can we live in a world with more people, more bad weather, and more **waste**, with dirty seas and **polluted air**? And then there are countries that are very, very rich, and countries that are very poor. There's a lot that must be done to make our world a better place to live, and we can all do something to help.

waste things that we throw away; to use something badly

polluted dirty; **pollute** to make dirty

air we take this in through our mouths and noses

READING CHECK

Tick (✔) the boxes to complete the sentences.

a Darwin was interested in…

1 ☑ plants and animals. **2** ☐ planets and stars. **3** ☐ ships and the sea.

b For his work on the *Beagle*, Darwin got…

1 ☐ a lot of money. **2** ☐ a little money. **3** ☐ no money.

c The *Beagle* travelled to…

1 ☐ North and South America.

2 ☐ South America and the Pacific.

3 ☐ Africa and India.

d Darwin thought that the beaks of finches changed because…

1 ☐ they ate different food.

2 ☐ they travelled around the world.

3 ☐ they were an old species.

e Most scientists in the 1830s thought that…

1 ☐ an old species could slowly change into a new species.

2 ☐ an old species could quickly change into a new species.

3 ☐ an old species could not change into a new species.

f Darwin's book was called…

1 ☐ *Animal Species on the Earth.*

2 ☐ *The Origin of the Earth.*

3 ☐ *On the Origin of Species.*

g When people began reading Darwin's book,…

1 ☐ most people agreed with the ideas in it.

2 ☐ some people felt cross about the ideas in it.

3 ☐ nobody understood it.

h Today, people think that Darwin's ideas…

1 ☐ were interesting but wrong.

2 ☐ were wrong and dangerous.

3 ☐ were right.

ACTIVITIES

WORD WORK

1 Match the words with the pictures.

beak	insect	land	planet	scientist	seeds

a ....insect........

b ....

c ....

d ....

e ....

f ....

2 Complete the sentences with the words from Activity 1.

a These small ....seeds........ will change into big plants.

b Some animals can live in water and on ....

c Saturn is a very big ....; it's much bigger than the Earth.

d An .... is a small animal with six legs.

e Isaac Newton was a famous English ....

f A .... is a part of a bird.

GUESS WHAT

The next chapter is about the environment. What do you know about it? Tick (✔) the boxes.

		True	False
a	In 1962, an American film star wrote an important book about the environment.	☐	☐
b	The first group which had 'green' in their name was from Germany.	☐	☐
c	The group World Wide Fund for Nature (WWF) started in the 1960s.	☐	☐
d	WWF helps people who have lost their homes in earthquakes.	☐	☐
e	Greenpeace was one of the first green groups in the world.	☐	☐
f	Greenpeace doesn't take money from anyone for its work.	☐	☐

2. Going green

pesticide something we use to kill insects and other small animals on plants

grow (*past* **grew**, **grown**) to get bigger

government the people who decide what happens in a country

appear to be suddenly in front of someone's eyes

In the 1950s and 1960s, people began to use a lot of **pesticides** on plants. Pesticides kill insects that eat vegetables and fruit. Without these insects, you can **grow** more vegetables and fruit, so you can make more money from them. Pesticides are still being used today, and the pesticide business makes more than two billion kilogrammes of pesticides every year. But where do all these pesticides go? They go into the ground, the rivers, the sea, the air, the plants and animals – and some pesticides even go into our food.

Rachel Carson and *Silent Spring*

Are pesticides good for you or bad for you? Does it matter? These questions worried a scientist, called Rachel Carson, who worked for the American **government** from 1936 to 1952. She thought pesticides were very dangerous and bad for the environment. They can kill the insects on the fruit and vegetable plants, so they can make other things ill, too – like animals, plants, and even people. Carson decided to write a book about this, and in 1962, her book *Silent Spring* **appeared**. In this book, she explained why she was worried about pesticides. Millions of people read the book and began to think and talk about these questions, too. Now you can buy food that is grown without pesticides, which is better for the environment and for your body.

Rachel Carson

Born: 1907 in the USA

Died: 1964 in the USA

Facts: At first, Carson wanted to be a writer. Next, she decided to work as a scientist. In the end, she was famous as a scientist and a writer.

The first Greens

You know the colour green, but do you know why some people and **organizations** call themselves green? Rachel Carson was very 'green' because she did a lot to help the environment. The most important thing for all Greens is **protecting** the environment – the plants, the animals, the ground, the air, and the sea. They also want to make life better for people without hurting the environment.

The first green **political** groups appeared in Australia and New Zealand in the early 1970s, and the first political group that used the name 'green' was Die Grünen (The Greens) in Germany in the early 1980s.

organization a group of people who work together to do something

protect to keep someone or something from danger; to take care of

political of or about the work of government

WWF and Greenpeace

There are many green organizations, too, like the World Wide Fund for Nature (WWF) and Greenpeace. These organizations don't belong to any government or business, and they don't make any money. People give them money, and they use it to help the environment in different ways.

WWF, which began in 1961, was one of the first 'green' organizations in the world. It works to **save** species that are in danger and to protect the environment. It also asks people to think about their lives and what they can do to help to protect the environment. More than five million people now belong to WWF in more than 100 countries.

Greenpeace began ten years after WWF. In 1971, a small group of people left Vancouver, Canada, on an old fishing boat called the *Phyllis Cormack*. They were going to the island of Amchitka, west of Alaska. Amchitka was the home of a lot of animals, but no people. It was also in a **part** of the world where earthquakes often happen. The people on the *Phyllis Cormack* were worried because the USA was using Amchitka for **nuclear tests**. 'Perhaps they won't do their tests if we're staying on the island,' they thought. 'Perhaps other people will hear about our **protest** and will tell the USA that they don't want the tests either.'

save to take someone or something out of danger

part some, but not all of something

nuclear we can make nuclear energy

test to do something to a thing or person to find out more information

protest something that you do which shows strongly that you don't like something; to say or show that you don't like something

The USA didn't stop the tests immediately, but this group of people went on protesting, and in 1972, the USA stopped the tests. The group were very happy about this, and they decided to go on protesting about the environment. They wanted to make a world that was green, with no **violence** between people or countries, so they took a new name – Greenpeace.

Now, more than fifty years later, nearly three million people belong to Greenpeace, and the organization has offices in more than forty countries. They make films, and they talk on the radio, TV, and the internet about things which are important to them, like **whale hunting**, nuclear waste, **rainforests**, and plastic. These are things they also protest about. They often go to places where bad or dangerous things are happening and try to stop them, but they don't use violence.

violence when people use violence they fight or hurt other people

whale

hunting / hunt to look for and kill animals

rainforest a hot forest where there is a lot of rain

ACTIVITIES

READING CHECK

1 Are these sentences about Greenpeace true or false? Tick (✔) the boxes.

		True	False
a	A group of people from Iceland started Greenpeace.	☐	☑
b	They went in a small plane to the island of Amchitka, near Alaska.	☐	☐
c	They were worried because the USA never uses violence.	☐	☐
d	In 1972, the USA stopped the tests.	☐	☐
e	Greenpeace wants to stop people watching whales.	☐	☐
f	Greenpeace often goes to places where dangerous things are happening to try to stop them.	☐	☐

2 Match the sentence halves.

a In 1936, Rachel Carson…
b In the 1950s and 1960s, people who worked on the land…
c In 1961, the group World Wide Fund for Nature (WWF)…
d In 1962, Rachel Carson…
e In the early 1970s, the first 'green' political groups…
f In the 1980s, Die Grünen…
g Today, the WWF…

1 works to protect our planet's environment.
2 began using pesticides.
3 began in Germany.
4 started their work to save wild animals.
5 wrote the book *Silent Spring*.
6 began working for the US government.
7 began in Australia and New Zealand.

WORD WORK

1 Reorder the letters in the rainforest to make words from Chapter 2.

ACTIVITIES

2 Complete the sentences with the words from Activity 1.

a We need to ....protect.......... the whales in our seas because they are in danger.
b Some .... groups don't belong to a government.
c People have cut down a lot of trees in the .... to make money.
d In the mountains, the .... is good because there isn't much traffic.
e Greenpeace is an .... that protects the environment.
f Greenpeace never uses .... when it protests about something.

3 Replace the underlined words with the correct words from the box.

appear hunting part pesticides ~~test~~

a They sometimes have to do a nuclear thing to find out more information. ....test..........
b Many green organizations don't like killing wild animals. ....
c In the mountains, storm clouds can often be suddenly in front of you. ....
d Some animal species only live in one piece of the world. ....
e Many people who grow food don't want to put something which kills insects on their plants. ....

GUESS WHAT

The next chapter is about climate change. What do you know about it? Tick (✓) the boxes.

	True	False
a Scientists think that climate change will soon stop.	☐	☐
b There will be more storms and dry, hot weather.	☐	☐
c More birds will travel around the world.	☐	☐
d The sea will be higher than it is now.	☐	☐
e Satellites and computers will help us to see how the Earth changes.	☐	☐

3. Climate change

climate the usual weather in a place over a year

become (*past* **became**) to begin to be

last to go on

problem something difficult

vice president the second most important person in a country

president the most important person in a country

The weather is always changing. It changes from one hour to the next, and from one day to the next. **Climate** is different from weather – it's the weather that a place usually has during the year every year. For example, a place can be hot in the summer and cold in the winter. This is its climate.

When people talk about climate change, they mean the usual weather in a place has changed. Perhaps the weather has **become** hotter or colder, wetter or drier, and this change will **last** over many years.

People have talked about climate change for a long time, but now more and more people are worried about it. One of the first people who tried to show the world that climate change is a big **problem** was Al Gore.

Al Gore and *An Inconvenient Truth*

Al Gore

Born: 1948 in the USA

Facts: Al Gore was **Vice President** of the USA from 1993 to 2001. He nearly became the **President** of the USA in 2000, but in the end George W. Bush became President.

damage to break or harm something

emergency when something terrible has happened and you must get help quickly

Al Gore was the Vice President of the USA for eight years, but perhaps this wasn't his most important job. In 2006, he made a film called *An Inconvenient Truth*. It's about climate change and how people – all of us – **damage** the environment, and it tells people what they can do to help. When Gore made the film, lots of people didn't think much about climate change. But millions of people watched it, and it changed how they thought. And now many people agree with him that the world is in a climate **emergency**.

Greenhouse gases

Scientists are seeing a lot of changes in our climate, but why? And what do these changes do to the environment? One thing that changes our climate is the **level** of **greenhouse gases** in the **atmosphere**. When we drive cars or travel on planes and trains, greenhouse gases like **carbon dioxide** (CO_2) go into the atmosphere. When **coal**, wood, or **oil** is burned to make your house warm, or burned in factories, this makes more greenhouse gases. Big **farms** with lots of animals put even more greenhouse gases, like methane, into the atmosphere.

There are now more greenhouse gases in the atmosphere than ever before, and the level of greenhouse gases is going up. These gases stop some of the sun's **energy** that hits the Earth going back into **space**, and this energy makes the Earth warmer.

level the sea level is the top of the sea

greenhouse gases when there is too much of these gases they can change the Earth's climate

atmosphere the gases around the Earth

carbon dioxide a greenhouse gas

coal

oil we get oil from the ground and use it to make things like plastic

farm a place where people have animals, or where they grow plants for food

energy something that gives us power

space there are many stars in space

A warmer Earth

Today, many scientists think that in the twenty-first **century** the Earth will perhaps become more than 2°C warmer because of **rising** greenhouse gases. In places where there are a lot of storms, the storms will become stronger and with more heavy rain than before. Hot, dry places will have hotter weather, and some rivers will get smaller.

The **temperature** of the sea is changing, too. It's now 1°C warmer than it was 140 years ago. Scientists say that by the end of this century, there won't be any ice in the Arctic in the summer; it will all **melt**.

What does this mean for the environment? Even a small change of 1°C can mean problems for plants and animals. Perhaps they can't live very easily in a warmer climate; perhaps the plants, which are the animals' food, will **disappear**. Perhaps some plants will grow earlier in the year, and there won't be any food when the animals have their babies.

Some birds travel from one part of the Earth to another every year, and they need places to stop, eat, and rest on the way. Climate change means that many of those places are disappearing under water or becoming too hot and dry. Then these birds will die because the journey will be too difficult for them.

century one hundred years

rise to come up

temperature how hot or cold something is

melt when ice turns to water

disappear to go away suddenly

Rising sea levels

The small Pacific island of Nuatambu, in the Solomon Islands, is half as big as it was in 2011. The island is slowly going under the sea because sea levels in the Pacific are rising. One Solomon Islander, ninety-four-year-old Sirilo Sutaroti, said, 'The sea has started to come…'. There were twenty-five families living on the island. Eleven of their houses are now under water.

Some scientists now say that by the end of the century, the world's sea level will go up by between 62 and 238 centimetres because the ice is melting. Possibly millions of people and animals will lose their homes, for example in countries like the islands of Indonesia, and Bangladesh which has nearly 25% of its land **less than** two metres above sea level. Big cities near the sea, like New York and Hong Kong, will have problems, too. When land disappears under the sea, it will be harder to grow food and to find **clean** water to drink.

less than not as much (as)

clean to stop something being dirty; when something is no longer dirty

The changes in our climate are changing the world for everyone. But what can we do about it? Thousands of scientists are working hard to find answers to this question, but we can all do something to help. Turn off lights, and try to walk when you can. If you do, you will help to make the levels of greenhouse gases in the atmosphere go down, and this will help the environment.

READING CHECK

Choose the correct words to complete the sentences.

a Al Gore *wrote a book / made a film* called *An Inconvenient Truth*.

b Scientists think that the Earth's temperature will *rise / come down* over the next few years.

c Greenhouse gases *help / damage* the environment.

d Cars and planes put greenhouse gases into *space / the atmosphere*.

e Scientists are worried because the ice in the Arctic is *melting / becoming harder*.

f Climate change means that food for animals will possibly grow *earlier / later in the year*.

g Many birds that try to fly across the world will probably change where they *live / die*.

h Part of the island of Nuatambu *will soon be / is already* under water.

i It will be harder for farmers to *grow / sell* food.

WORD WORK

1 Complete the crossword puzzle with words from Chapter 3.

2 Complete the sentences with the words from Activity 1.

- **a** On our ....farm.......... , we grow potatoes and carrots.
- **b** The most important person in the USA is the ....
- **c** We need to stop burning .... because it's bad for the environment.
- **d** Look at my bedroom – it's nice and .... !
- **e** My parents were born in the twentieth ....
- **f** The journey to my friend's house isn't very long; it's .... than one hour.
- **g** Scientists think that some islands will .... because the sea level is rising.
- **h** If he eats that old food, he will .... ill.
- **i** My father made this table well. I think that it will .... for many years.

GUESS WHAT

The next chapter is about tropical rainforests. What do you know about them? Tick (✔) the boxes.

	True	False
a In tropical rainforests, it rains all year.	☐	☐
b Trees in rainforests can be up to sixty metres tall.	☐	☐
c Most of the flowers and fruits in the rainforest grow on the ground.	☐	☐
d More than 70% of the world's animal species live in the rainforest.	☐	☐
e When we clean our homes, we use things that come from the rainforest.	☐	☐
f Cutting down the rainforest helps the climate in other parts of the world.	☐	☐

tropical rainforest

4. Tropical rainforests

tropical from the hottest part of the world

roof the top part of something

oxygen something in the air; animals need oxygen to live

drought when there is little or no rain for a long time

There are **tropical** rainforests in Central and South America, West and Central Africa, Southeast Asia and Australia. Some tropical rainforests get a lot of rain all year, but some only get rain for a few months of the year. Tropical rainforests are near the hottest parts of the planet, so they're warm, too – usually between 20°C and 35°C. Some of the world's biggest rivers, like the Amazon, are in rainforests.

At the top of a rainforest, there are very tall trees which grow up to sixty metres tall. Below them the tops of smaller trees come together like a **roof** of leaves, called a canopy. Here you find bright flowers and fruits, and many birds and other animals come to eat them. Below this there are smaller trees, and when you get to the ground it's dark, because the leaves of the trees stop a lot of the light from the sun.

Why do we need rainforests?

Rainforests help to give us **oxygen**. Driving cars and burning wood puts carbon dioxide into the air; and trees take in carbon dioxide from the air and use it to make oxygen. This helps to stop climate change and weather problems like floods and **droughts**.

There are more than 40,000 plant species in the Amazon. Tropical rainforests are the home of 50% of the animal species in the world, too.

medicine
something you eat or drink to make you better when you are ill

Rainforests in danger

In any forest, old trees die, and new ones grow in their place – but sometimes people **cut down** or burn all the trees in a forest. This is called **deforestation**, and it's one of the biggest problems for rainforests today. Sometimes people do this because they want the wood, and sometimes they want to use the land for **farming**. In the past, it was usually farmers who cut down the trees, but today big businesses are doing it to make new or bigger farms. They can make a lot of money from these.

Scientists think that every year, an **area** of rainforest as big as the country of Panama disappears because of deforestation. An area as big as thirty football fields of rainforest disappears every minute. We have seen why rainforests are so important, so this is a big problem for everyone. Scientists say that deforestation in the Amazon rainforest in South America can **affect** the climate in other parts of the world as far away as France.

cut down when you cut down a tree and then it falls

deforestation taking away the trees from a place

farming growing plants and animals for food

area a piece of land

affect to change something or someone

Burning the rainforest to **remove** the trees brings other problems. Because of smoke from the fires, people can become ill, or even die. In Southeast Asia, about 100,000 people die each year from problems that come from this smoke. And burning the trees means that more greenhouse gases go into the air, which means more climate change.

Deforestation also hurts or kills animals and plants because they lose their homes and food. And without the trees, the land can get too hot for them to live on.

The golden toads

People first saw the Monteverde golden **toad** in the 1960s in a rainforest in Costa Rica. The **male** toads were only five centimetres long, and they were very bright orange. The **female** toads were a little bigger, and they were black with bright red and yellow **spots**.

Monteverde golden toads

Each year in April, when it rains a lot, male and female toads met in **pools** of water in the rainforest. The female toads left their eggs in the pools, and the eggs soon grew into young toads. Then the toads disappeared into the rainforest for another year.

There were hundreds of golden toads in the 1960s, but in 1988, scientists looked for the toads and only found ten. In 1989, they found just one – and since then nobody has seen any golden toads.

What happened to the toads? Some people say that climate change killed the toads; others say that it was deforestation or pesticides that killed them. Nobody knows, but today toads in other countries are disappearing, too. Is it too late for the toads of the world?

remove to take away

toad a small animal with four legs that spends time on land and in water

male an animal that can't make eggs or have babies

female an animal that can make eggs and have babies

spot a circle of a different colour

pool water on the ground

READING CHECK

Are the sentences true or false? Tick (✓) the boxes.

		True	False
a	There are some tropical rainforests in Australia.	✓	☐
b	In tropical rainforests the highest temperature is usually about 35°C.	☐	☐
c	There is less light near the canopy than on the ground.	☐	☐
d	Trees take in oxygen and make carbon dioxide.	☐	☐
e	We use rainforest plants to make many of our medicines.	☐	☐
f	Coffee and chocolate come from plants that first grew in the rainforest.	☐	☐
g	Some big businesses cut down the rainforests for farming.	☐	☐
h	Big fires can make people ill because of the smoke.	☐	☐
i	Nobody has seen any golden toads in Costa Rica since 1979.	☐	☐

WORD WORK

1 Find and circle new words from Chapter 4.

2 Complete the sentences with the words from Activity 1.

- **a** There is a big ......area...... of land near my house which doesn't belong to anybody.
- **b** A .... animal can't have babies.
- **c** The rain is coming into my bedroom because there is a hole in our ....
- **d** The problems that happen from climate change will .... everyone in the world.
- **e** There is a little .... in our garden, where birds come to drink.
- **f** In many bird species, the male birds are more colourful than the .... birds.
- **g** When deforestation happens, people .... trees from part of a forest.
- **h** During a ...., many plants die because there is no water.

GUESS WHAT

The next chapter is about making special places to protect animals. Can you guess the answers to these questions? Tick (✓) the boxes.

a What was the number of bison in North America in the early 1800s?

1 ☐ 60 million **2** ☐ 100 million **3** ☐ 120 million

b What was the number of bison in North America in 1895?

1 ☐ 200 **2** ☐ 800 **3** ☐ 1,500

c What is the number of bison in North America today?

1 ☐ 5,000 **2** ☐ 50,000 **3** ☐ 500,000

d Which country has a park to protect jaguars?

1 ☐ Belize **2** ☐ Chile **3** ☐ Nepal

e How much of the world's land is special land where animals are not in danger?

1 ☐ 5% **2** ☐ 10% **3** ☐ 15%

bison

jaguar

national park

5. Making safe places

space an area; a place that is big enough

extinct when all of a species dies

bison a big animal with four legs and big horns

horn

Native American a person who lived in America before white people arrived

skin what is on the outside of an animal's body

canoe a long, narrow boat

bone a hard, white thing inside an animal's body

People need **space** to live, work, and play, and animals need space, too. Sometimes it's difficult to find this space. Just think about the changes in the number of people on the Earth. In the year 1100, there were 320 million people on the planet. The number of people slowly grew to 1.6 billion (1,600 million) by 1900, but by 2020 there were nearly 7.8 billion people. Every year there are more and more people, so we build more and more places for them to live and work. This means there is less space for the wild animals that lived on this land before we did.

People make other problems for wild animals, too. They kill these animals because they're dangerous, or because they want their body parts. Many animal species are **extinct** or nearly extinct because people have hunted them too much.

The North American bison

North American **bison** are very big, heavy animals – about 2,000 kilograms – with **horns** that are nearly two metres across. The first bison came to North America from Asia about 100,000 years ago. The **Native Americans** began to hunt bison thousands of years ago. They used the bison's **skins** to make clothes, homes, and **canoes**, and with the **bones**, they made things to fight with.

When Europeans came to North America they, too, began to kill bison. They wanted the strong skins to use and sell, and they also thought that bison were a danger to their farm animals. The Europeans enjoyed hunting, too – you could even pay to ride on a train and shoot bison all day.

national park a large piece of beautiful land that the government looks after

In the early 1800s, there were about 60 million bison across North America. But by 1895, there were only about 800 of them. When there are only a small number of one species, it's very easy for the species to become extinct. People needed to help the bison before it was too late.

In 1902, there were around twenty bison in Yellowstone **National Park**. The government said that no one could hunt the bison there now; the bison could live there without danger. Over many years, the number of bison grew, and there are about 500,000 bison in North America today.

John Muir and Yosemite National Park

You can find national parks all around the world. These big spaces are very special because all the animals and plants in them are protected. People can't hurt the animals or cut down the trees there. They can only go to national parks to enjoy them. In 1872, Yellowstone was the first area in the USA to become a national park. It was followed by Yosemite, and the person who worked the hardest to make this national park was John Muir.

John Muir

Born: 1838 in Scotland

Died: 1914 in the USA

Facts: When he was twenty-nine, he walked 1,600 kilometres across the USA.

In 1863, John Muir began travelling across the USA and Canada, and in 1868, he arrived in California. When he saw the beautiful mountains of the Sierra Nevada for the first time, he thought that they were wonderful. He went on travelling and writing there for years, telling people about the mountains and the wild country, and asking them to enjoy and protect these special places.

Farm animals, like sheep and cows, damaged the mountain forests, and this worried Muir. He wrote to newspapers and gave talks about the problem. At last, in 1890, the US government made Yosemite National Park. Muir helped to make four more national parks, wrote many books about them, and began the Sierra Club to help protect wild places. People called him 'the father of our national parks'. He went on doing this work until he died.

safe not dangerous

university people study here after they finish school

jaguar

Alan Rabinowitz and the jaguars

Like John Muir, Alan Rabinowitz worked very hard to make a **safe** place for animals. He studied animals at **university** and then, in 1979, he got a job studying a big wild cat called the **jaguar** in Belize, in Central America.

Alan Rabinowitz

Born: 1953 in the USA

Died: 2018 in the USA

Facts: When Rabinowitz was a child, he couldn't talk very well, and he didn't like speaking to people. But he loved animals, and it was easier for him to talk to them.

Rabinowitz's plan was to catch jaguars and put radios on them, so that he could learn about how they lived. He was the first person to study jaguars like this, and he learned that there were many dangers for jaguars, like hunting. He didn't want the jaguars to become extinct, so he talked to the government of Belize. They agreed to make a safe space for the jaguars, called Cockscomb Basin Wildlife Sanctuary. Now, Cockscomb is the biggest forest that is safe for animals in all of Central America.

National parks today

Nearly 15% of the world's land is now protected, but there are new problems for national parks because of climate change. In Australia, for example, there is a national park around the Great Barrier Reef. It protects the beautiful **coral reef** and all the life in it. But climate change means warmer sea water and more carbon dioxide, so the coral loses its colour, and sometimes it can't grow, or it dies.

coral reef a beautiful hard thing under the sea that looks like a plant; small animals live in it

ACTIVITIES

READING CHECK

Match the sentence halves.

a Native Americans...
b Europeans thought that bison...
c John Muir...
d The government of the USA...
e Alan Rabinowitz...
f The government of Belize...

1 was called 'the father of our national parks' by many Americans.
2 studied jaguars in Belize for five years.
3 could harm their farm animals.
4 used the skins of bison to make clothes, homes, and canoes.
5 made a big park in Central America to protect animals.
6 made Yosemite National Park in 1890.

WORD WORK

1 Reorder the letters to make words from Chapter 5.

ACTIVITIES

2 Match the definitions with words from Activity 1.

a Some of the first people who lived in North America. Native Americans
b People can go here to study after they have finished school. ....
c A long, narrow boat; people often use it on rivers. ....
d Hard things that are inside the body of a person or animal. ....
e A large area of land where animals can be safe. ....
f This is on the outside of the body of a person or animal. ....
g A beautiful, hard thing under the sea; plants and fish live here. ....
h An area. ....

GUESS WHAT

In the next chapter, you will read about the world's oceans and some animals that live there. What do you know about them? Tick (✔) the boxes.

		True	False
a	The temperature of the sea water near Antarctica can be as cold as -10°C.	☐	☐
b	There are more than fifteen different species of penguin in the world.	☐	☐
c	All adult penguins have black backs and white fronts.	☐	☐
d	Emperor penguins can't stay under water for more than ten minutes.	☐	☐
e	Polar bears can swim through the water at ten kilometres per hour.	☐	☐
f	People began hunting whales thousands of years ago.	☐	☐

Emperor penguin

polar bear

whale

6. The oceans

ocean a large sea

penguin a bird that lives in cold places; it can't fly

If you go high up into the air and look down at the Earth, the colour you will see most is blue. This is because more than 70% of the Earth is water. In many places, the world's **oceans** are over 3,500 metres deep. In the warmest places, the water in the oceans can be 30°C, but in the icy waters near Antarctica, it can be as cold as -2°C. There are hundreds of different animal species in the sea, from very little animals up to very big animals like the blue whale.

Penguins

In 1498, the Portuguese traveller Vasco da Gama was surprised to see some strange animals in the Atlantic Ocean, far from land. They were birds that couldn't fly, but swam like fish, and they made a noise like a wild horse. What were these strange things? They were **penguins**!

There are between seventeen and twenty penguin species in the world today. Two penguin species – the Adélie and Emperor – live in Antarctica, and Emperor penguins can stay alive when it's as cold as -50°C. The other penguin species also live in the southern oceans, and they spend most of their time – sometimes as much as 75% of it – in the sea.

All adult penguins have black backs and white fronts; this helps to protect them when they are in the sea because it's difficult to see these colours from above or below. But different species have different colours on their heads, and penguins can be as small as a chicken or as big as a young child.

Penguins stopped flying and began to swim under the water about 50 million years ago, and their bodies have slowly changed. Now, the water moves easily over their bodies, and they can travel very fast – up to about thirty-five kilometres per hour. They can also travel a long way. Emperor penguins, for example, can stay at sea for a month and travel nearly 1,600 kilometres!

Penguins are very good at **diving**, too. Emperor penguins can stay under water for more than twenty minutes and can dive down more than 550 metres. Penguins can see very well, both in the air and in the water, and they have heavy bones that help them to dive down deep.

dive / diving to swim under water

Penguins aren't usually afraid of people; they're often interested, and will come to see what people are doing. Because of this, it has been easy in the past for people to catch them or take their eggs. For example, in 1867 in the Falkland Islands (las Islas Malvinas), people killed 405,000 penguins to get the oil from their bodies. The birds nearly became extinct on the islands. People don't hunt penguins for oil today, but there are different dangers for these birds.

Plastic, like plastic bags and bottles that go into the oceans, can hurt or kill the animals that live there. When scientists look inside penguins' bodies, they often find very small pieces of plastic or 'microplastic'.

Climate change is dangerous for penguins, too. Penguins eat a lot of a small animal called **krill**, which can only live in cold water. Warmer seas mean less food for the penguins, so they can become very hungry and die.

For the penguins that live in Antarctica, there's another problem from climate change. When the seas get warmer, the sea ice begins to disappear, and there's less space for these birds to make their homes. The World Wide Fund for Nature (WWF) says that if the world temperatures go up by 2°C by 2050, perhaps 50% of Emperor penguins and 75% of Adélie penguins will disappear. Will warmer temperatures mean the end for these wonderful birds?

krill

Polar bears

It's not only penguins that are in danger from climate change. There have been **polar bears** in the Arctic for thousands of years. They are often two metres tall or more, and as heavy as 600 kilogrammes. Their big feet help them to walk across snow and ice, and they're very good swimmers, travelling at ten kilometres per hour through the water.

The most important food for polar bears is **seals**. In winter, polar bears wait quietly near holes in the ice, and when a seal comes up for air, the polar bear catches it. In summer, there's no ice there, so the polar bears live on land. They can't catch seals on land, so they live with little or no food in the summer.

But things are changing because of climate change. The Arctic ice is melting earlier in the year now – perhaps three weeks earlier. Then, in the winter, the hungry bears have to wait longer before there's ice again. The polar bears now have much less time to hunt seals. Some scientists say that polar bears are now on land for thirty days more each year than in the past. This is making polar bears thinner, and they aren't as heavy. They don't have as many babies, and these babies are smaller than before.

There is another problem, too. Polar bears now look for food in towns more often, and sometimes polar bears or people die because of this. Scientists are watching polar bears carefully, but the **future** doesn't look good for these beautiful bears.

polar bear a big white bear that lives in cold places

seal

future the time that will come

Whales

Whales are very clever animals which usually live in groups and hunt together. Most whales are very big – the blue whale can grow to 30 metres long; it's the biggest animal in the world! But whales are in danger, too, and six species are nearly extinct.

Whales need to come to the top of the ocean to get air. This makes it easier for people to hunt them for their meat, oil, and bones. People have done this for thousands of years. Today, only a few countries kill whales like this, but still thousands of whales die each year. In some of these places, people say that they've always hunted whales and that it's a part of their way of life. But other people want to protect the whales and think it's wrong for anyone to hunt them.

There's another way of making money from whales. Every year, millions of people all over the world go out in boats to watch them. Whale-watching makes billions of dollars a year, but it brings problems, too. The boats can be too loud for the whales or get too near to them. Sometimes boats can even hit the whales. The boats make the water dirtier, too which can make the whales ill.

The longest chase

Organizations like Greenpeace and WWF protect whales and other animals in the ocean. They never use violence, but another organization called Sea Shepherd helps these animals in a different way.

On 17 December 2014, a Sea Shepherd ship began to follow another ship called *Thunder*. *Thunder* was using **illegal nets** to catch an expensive fish called toothfish. Sea Shepherd **chased** *Thunder* from Antarctica to Africa. The ships nearly crashed into each other, and Sea Shepherd cut *Thunder's* nets, but the chase still went on. Finally, on 6 April 2015, the **captain** of *Thunder* asked Sea Shepherd for help because *Thunder* was **sinking**. The *Thunder* captain and the other people from *Thunder* got onto the Sea Shepherd boats, and *Thunder* sank. The captain and two other men from *Thunder* had to pay 17 million dollars and go to prison for two to three years. The chase went on for 110 days and for 16,000 kilometres. It was the longest sea chase ever.

Sea Shepherd began in Canada in 1977, and now people work for Sea Shepherd in over twenty countries around the world. They fight to stop illegal hunting and to protect the oceans.

illegal if something is illegal, the rules of a country say you can't do it

net an open bag with small holes that you use to catch fish

chase to follow something to try to catch it

captain the most important person on a ship

sink (*past* **sank**) to go to the bottom of the sea

ACTIVITIES

READING CHECK

1 Correct one mistake in each sentence.

- **a** ~~Five~~ Two penguin species live in Antarctica.
- **b** Different penguin species have different colours on their feet.
- **c** Penguins can swim, but they can't dive.
- **d** Many polar bears are about four metres tall.
- **e** Seals come up through holes in the ice for food.
- **f** Millions of people go out in boats every year to watch penguins.
- **g** The ship *Thunder* used illegal guns to try to catch toothfish.

2 Match the sentence halves.

a There is water over more than…	**1** penguins in the Atlantic Ocean.
b The water temperature in the oceans…	**2** 70% of the Earth.
c In 1498, the traveller Vasco da Gama saw…	**3** Emperor and Adélie penguins in danger.
d Less sea ice in Antarctica will put…	**4** whales for their meat, oil, and bones.
e A few countries still hunt…	**5** can be as high as 30°C in some places.

WORD WORK

1 Complete the puzzle with words from Chapter 6. What's the mystery word?

- **1** a very big sea
- **2** to follow something quickly when you want to catch it
- **3** black and white birds
- **4** a thing that people use to catch fish
- **5** when a country's laws say that you can't do it
- **6** to swim under water
- **7** to fall down to the bottom of the sea

Mystery word: ....

2 Complete the sentences with the words from Activity 1.

a The blue whale is the biggest animal in the ......ocean...... .

b Look – there's a big fish in the fisherman's .... !

c If I throw this heavy bag into the water, it will ....

d The police are always trying to .... criminals.

e I can swim, and I can also ....

f The sailors on the ship work hard for their ....

g In many countries, smoking is .... in restaurants.

h .... like eating krill.

GUESS WHAT

The next chapter is about energy and the accidents that can happen when getting it. What do you know about this? Tick (✔) the boxes.

	True	False
a We get oil from deep under the ground.	☐	☐
b If oil goes into the sea, it disappears quickly.	☐	☐
c There has only been one bad oil accident since 2010.	☐	☐
d Chernobyl is a large town in Russia.	☐	☐
e There was a terrible accident in Chernobyl in 1986.	☐	☐
f Thousands of people who lived in or near Chernobyl had to leave their homes.	☐	☐
g There was a nuclear accident in Fukushima.	☐	☐
h The land near the Fukushima power plant still isn't clean.	☐	☐

nuclear accident at Fukushima power plant, 2011

7. Energy and its cost

People need energy – lots of it. We need it for our homes and computers, our cars, our shops, and our factories. We can't live without energy. But can we get energy safely and cleanly? And what happens if something goes wrong?

Oil and *Deepwater Horizon*

A lot of our energy comes from oil, and one of the best places to find oil is under the sea. For more than a hundred years, people have built big oil rigs in the water to get to the oil. *Deepwater Horizon* was a big oil rig in the Gulf of Mexico. It belonged to the BP oil **company**. In September 2009, it made the deepest oil **well** in the world, more than 10,000 metres under the sea. But the next year, the name *Deepwater Horizon* was suddenly in the news all over the world for the wrong reasons.

At 9.50 p.m. on the night of 20 April 2010, there was an **explosion** on *Deepwater Horizon*. Soon after this, there was a fire. Eleven workers on the rig died, and many others were hurt. Boats soon came to take them to hospital, and to take the other workers to a safe place. People worked hard to stop the fire, but on 22 April 2010, the rig disappeared under the sea.

company a business

well a deep hole where people can get water or oil

explosion when something breaks into pieces with a very loud noise

Deepwater Horizon oil rig

This was only the start of the **disaster**. People tried to stop the oil coming out of the well and into the sea, but it was eighty-seven days before the oil stopped. It was the biggest oil-rig accident ever. Scientists think that about 630 million litres of oil went into the sea. Millions of sea animals and plants died, and eight different national parks were in danger from the oil. Years after the disaster, the oil still affects living things in the Gulf of Mexico. It will be a long, long time before all the oil from *Deepwater Horizon* disappears.

For the people who live near the Gulf, it was a disaster, too. Fishermen couldn't go to sea to catch fish, and visitors stayed away from some of the beaches for many years. Then there were **health** problems for people who helped to clean the sea and the beaches, and also for people who lived there. Some doctors think that this was because of the oil, or because of what they used to clean and remove the oil from the beaches.

After the disaster, people talked a lot about how to make things safer, and they changed some things on oil rigs. But in November 2012, there was another fire on an oil rig in the Gulf of Mexico, and three people died.

disaster something very bad that happens and that may hurt or kill a lot of people

health how well and strong a person is

Nuclear power disasters

electricity energy that comes along wires and makes things work; computers and TVs use electricity

power plant a building where power/electricity is made

power energy, like electricity, that makes something work

radioactive material something dangerous that you can find at a power plant

cover this goes on top of something

For billions of people everywhere, **electricity** is a very important kind of energy. When scientists first made plans for nuclear **power plants** in the 1950s, a lot of people thought that this was the best way to make electricity. They thought nuclear **power** was clean and safe, and that it didn't make big changes in the land. Later people began to see it in a different way.

Many people know the name 'Chernobyl'. In April 1986, an accident at the nuclear power plant in this small town in Ukraine killed thirty-one people. **Radioactive material** went out of the power plant and up into the air. Because of this, many more people got ill in the years that followed, and some of them died. Thousands of people had to leave their homes, too, because the area around Chernobyl wasn't safe.

The USA, Russia, Ukraine, and some other European countries worked together to make a very big **cover** to put over the Chernobyl power plant, and thirty years later, in November 2016, they put the cover in place. Scientists want the radioactive material to stay inside, and they will go on watching the power plant for many years.

Chernobyl cover

After Chernobyl nuclear power disaster, 1986

In 2011, the world's second big nuclear accident happened in Fukushima in Japan. This time a large earthquake and a **tsunami** damaged the power plant, and then there were explosions inside. Radioactive material went into the air. Thousands of people had to leave the land nearest to the power plant because of the danger.

Scientists think that the government will have to remove more than 19 million metres of **soil** from the land around the Fukushima power plant to make it safe again. That will cost a lot of money. And what do you do with the soil? Nobody wants to have thousands of bags of radioactive soil near their homes or offices.

Tsutomu Ueno is a farmer who lives in Aizu, west of the Fukushima power plant. The wind didn't take much radioactive material to Aizu, and the fruit and rice that he grows are safe. But he can't get much money for them because people still worry about **radiation**. He wants to go on farming, but it's hard for him to make money. The problems from nuclear disasters go on for a long time after the accidents happen.

tsunami a very big wave that comes after an earthquake

soil plants grow in soil; we find it on the ground

radiation a dangerous energy that can hurt people's health

Coal

mine to get coal from under the ground; a place under the ground where people work to get coal

rock the dry, hard part of the Earth; a very big stone

machine something that does work for people

More than two thousand years ago, long before people used oil or got electricity from nuclear power plants, they used coal to make their houses warm. From the eighteenth century, people began to use it more and more, but many problems come from burning coal. It pollutes the air, which makes people ill, and it makes more greenhouse gases, which makes the climate change.

Coal comes from under the ground, and getting it from there is difficult. Today we **mine** coal in many countries, and more than 40% of coal comes from China. Coal mining can be very dangerous; sometimes hundreds of people die because of fires, explosions, and falling **rocks** in the mines.

Coal mining also affects the environment. Today, about 40% of coal mining is done above the ground. Big **machines** remove trees, plants, and even mountains, so people can get to the coal under them. This changes the land. Where once there were trees and animals, now there are just rocks. In parts of the USA, big areas of land with mountains have disappeared to make coal mines. Animals lose their homes, rivers become polluted, and the air becomes polluted, too.

Clean energy for the future?

In a lot of countries, people have begun to use other ways of making electricity – from wind, for example, or from the sea or the sun. These are clean and safe for the environment. But some countries are planning and building new nuclear power plants, and others are burning more coal than ever before.

Every time we make or use energy, it affects the environment in some way. How are we going to get energy in the future? We must think about the environment when we decide.

ACTIVITIES

READING CHECK

Tick (✔) the correct answers to complete the sentences.

a The *Deepwater Horizon* disaster happened in…
1 ☐ 2010. **2** ☐ 2014. **3** ☐ 2018.

b During the disaster, the sea became polluted with…
1 ☐ coal dust. **2** ☐ oil. **3** ☐ radioactive material.

c The accident at Chernobyl happened at…
1 ☐ a nuclear power plant. **2** ☐ a mine. **3** ☐ an oil rig.

d After the accident, many governments worked together to…
1 ☐ build new homes there. **2** ☐ make cleaner energy for the town.
3 ☐ build a big cover for the power plant.

e In Fukushima, … damaged the power plant.
1 ☐ bad storms and a big fire **2** ☐ an earthquake and a tsunami
3 ☐ a plane crash

f Now, a big problem for the people of Fukushima is the radioactive…
1 ☐ coal. **2** ☐ water. **3** ☐ soil.

g More than … of the world's coal is mined from above the ground.
1 ☐ 80% **2** ☐ 40% **3** ☐ 60%

h Getting energy from … can pollute the air around us.
1 ☐ wind power **2** ☐ burning coal **3** ☐ the sun

WORD WORK

1 Complete the sentences with the words from the box.

cover	health	machine	rock	well

a There's an interesting fossil in that ....
b Before you can get oil from the ground, you need to dig a deep ....
c Eating lots of fruit and vegetables is good for your ....
d It's going to be cold tonight, so I have put a .... over the tomato plants.
e The factory has bought a new .... which can make parts more quickly.

2 Use the shapes to make words from Chapter 7. Then complete the sentences.

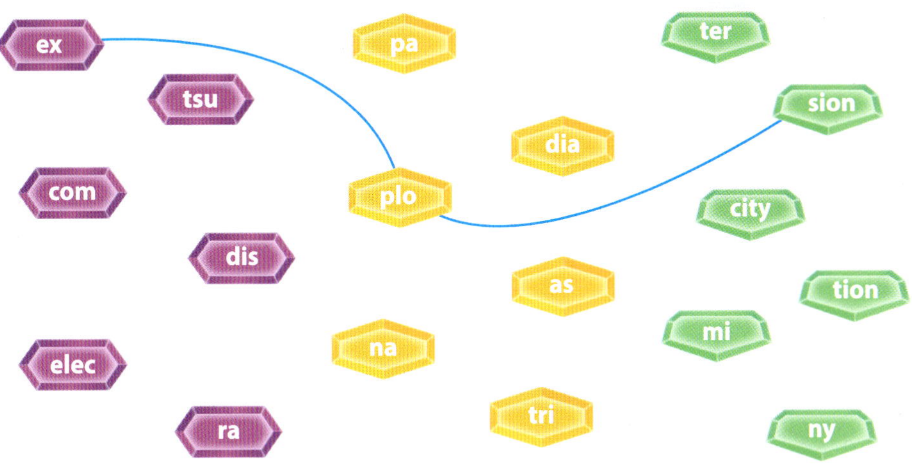

a The accident on *Deepwater Horizon* began with an explosion.

b The BP oil .... had to pay a lot of money after the accident on *Deepwater Horizon*.

c People can become ill if there are high levels of ....

d We use .... every day for the lights and machines in our houses.

e The nuclear .... in Chernobyl affected many different countries.

f A .... is when big waves from the sea come into land very quickly, after an earthquake.

GUESS WHAT

The next chapter is about the future of our planet. What do you think you will read about? Tick (✓) four boxes.

- **a** ☐ eating less meat
- **b** ☐ using clean energy
- **c** ☐ making clothes from food
- **d** ☐ climate change protests
- **e** ☐ travelling by whale
- **f** ☐ building 'green' houses
- **g** ☐ making plastic trees
- **h** ☐ protecting old buildings
- **i** ☐ sending waste into space

8. A greener future?

What can we do to protect our environment? How can we make a greener future for our planet? How can we stop putting dangerous gases into the atmosphere? People are talking about these questions a lot, and they're spending a lot of time and money to try to find answers.

Carbon footprint

When you walk across a floor with wet feet, you can see your **footprints** behind you; they show where you have been. In the same way, we all have a **carbon footprint** which shows how many greenhouse gases a person makes as they live their life. It's called a carbon footprint because one of the most important greenhouse gases is carbon dioxide.

footprint a mark that your foot or shoe makes on the ground or floor

carbon footprint the amount of carbon one person puts into the atmosphere

second-hand something that someone has used before

We can't see our carbon footprint, but it's there. If we travel by car a lot, eat a lot of meat from animals from big farms, waste food, and buy or use many new things, we have a bigger carbon footprint. If we walk everywhere, eat food made from plants that grow close to our home, and buy **second-hand** things, we have a smaller carbon footprint.

Anyone can find out their carbon footprint. A lot of websites can help you to do it. You answer questions about your home, your travel, and the food that you eat, and the website will tell you about your carbon footprint: is it big or small? How can you make it smaller? Here are some ideas.

recycle use something again; make something new using waste

throw away put something away because you don't want it

offset when you do something good after doing something bad

- Don't take the car – get the train or bus, or, even better, walk or ride a bicycle. If you have to drive, go with other people when you can. Try not to drive in busy places: cars put a lot more dangerous gases into the air when they're stopping and starting all the time.
- If you have to fly, do it less often and don't go far.
- Turn off computers, TVs, phones, and lights when you're not using them.
- Buy food that comes from places close to your home.
- Buy just the food that you need, and use it all – don't waste good food.
- **Recycle** to stop waste.
- Don't buy too many new clothes. Don't **throw away** your old clothes – mend them, make new things with them, sell them, or take them to a second-hand shop.
- Eat more fruit, vegetables, and food made of plants, and eat less meat.
- Don't use a lot of water when you wash.
- Don't buy water in plastic bottles, or drinks in plastic cups. Carry a water bottle and a coffee cup, and use them again.
- Buy green electricity – electricity from the wind, the sun, or the sea.
- **Offset** your carbon footprint. Give money to organizations that work to stop deforestation or make clean energy. There are websites which can show you how much money to give, for example, every time you fly somewhere.

These are small things, so will they help? Well, there are billions of people on the planet. And billions of people doing small things can make the future look very different.

Greta Thunberg and student protests

Some people think that they need to do more than just small things to protect our environment. In October 2018, fifteen-year-old Greta Thunberg from Sweden began to protest about climate change. She stopped going to school on Fridays and sat outside the Swedish government buildings. She wanted the government to do more – much more – to stop climate change. Other students heard about her protest and began to do the same. Protests began in other countries and became bigger.

Greta Thunberg, 2018

Greta Thunberg

Born: 2003 in Sweden

Facts: Greta's mother is a singer who travelled around the world. When Greta became worried about climate change, her mother stopped flying and her father stopped eating meat.

On 20 September 2019, only eleven months after Greta started her protest, millions of people around the world stayed away from work and school for the day to protest about climate change. Greta was doing something very important. Because of one young person, lots of other people decided to protest, too. Greta now travels around the world (but not by plane) and goes to important meetings to ask the governments of the world to do more to stop climate change.

Greta Thunberg, 2021

Becoming carbon neutral

For years now, governments from many countries around the world have come together to talk about the problems of the environment. Some of these governments are now talking about when their countries will help the environment by becoming **carbon neutral**.

It isn't easy for countries to become carbon neutral, and many people and scientists think that countries need to do a lot more, and faster. But some countries are trying to find new ways of living and working that are better for the environment.

Cities use 78% of the energy that we make, and they put more than 60% of the greenhouse gases into the air, so it's very important that cities change fast. In 2012, the Copenhagen city government said that they wanted their city to be carbon neutral by 2025, which is much sooner than most other cities. In 2012, many people said that this wasn't possible. But Copenhagen's carbon footprint is now much smaller, and the city is still changing. So how is it doing this?

Copenhagen is growing, but the city government doesn't want people to live outside the city and travel a long way to work or school. So it's changing the old parts of the city, like Nordhavn, into new places with new schools, new shops and new sports centres, and it's building **sustainable** homes there, too. There are new underground trains, and the city also has more than 350 kilometres of **cycle lanes**, so people travel less by car.

carbon neutral or 'carbon 0' is when you don't put dangerous greenhouse gases into the atmosphere

sustainable something is sustainable if it doesn't damage the environment

cycle lane a road for bicycles

The Copenhagen city government is also building new power plants to get clean energy, for example from the wind and the sun. At the new ARC power plant in the city, which makes waste into energy, people can **ski** down the side of the building! The government is trying to help our planet, and at the same time it's trying to make life better for people.

Before the ARC power plant was made, scientists had to work very hard to understand how they could change waste into energy. And all around the world, scientists are still working hard to find answers to the problem of climate change. For example, in 2013, scientists grew meat in a **lab** for the first time. It was very expensive to do this then. But now lots of companies are trying to find cheaper ways to make meat in a lab.

Scientists are also trying to make **hydrogen** cheaply and easily. When we use hydrogen to get electricity, or in cars and buses, it doesn't put greenhouse gases into the air.

Scientists want to find better ways to **store** energy from the wind, the sea, and the sun, too. And they are trying to understand how we can take carbon dioxide from power plants and store it under the ground or change it into something useful.

ski

lab a room where a scientist works

hydrogen a 'green' gas

store to have in one place

In Israel, scientists think that they have found out how to change special **bacteria** in a way that will perhaps help the environment. These bacteria usually eat sugar, but the scientists have changed them, so they now eat carbon dioxide. In the future, scientists can perhaps use these bacteria to make food or **fuel** that doesn't put carbon dioxide into the air – or even to make food that takes carbon dioxide out of it!

If scientists go on doing work like this, and if every person in the world begins to live in a more sustainable way, will it be possible to have a greener planet? Is the future going to get better or worse, or stay the same? What do you think? What will you do?

bacteria very small things that live in air, water, earth, plants, and animals

fuel anything you burn to make energy/power

READING CHECK

Complete the sentences with the words from the box.

cars	cities	houses	hydrogen	~~plants~~	plastic	protest	waste

a We have a smaller carbon footprint if we eat more food that comes from plants.

b When we need to travel somewhere, we can try not to use our ……………… .

c Cups that are made of ……………… are bad for our planet.

d Greta Thunberg started a climate change ……………… when she began sitting outside the Government buildings every Friday.

e More than half of all the greenhouse gases in the air come from our ……………… .

f In Copenhagen, there is a power plant which makes energy from ……………… .

g Nordhavn, in Copenhagen, has sustainable ……………… – which don't use much energy.

h Making electricity from ……………… is good for the environment.

WORD WORK

1 Look at the pictures and write the words.

a lab

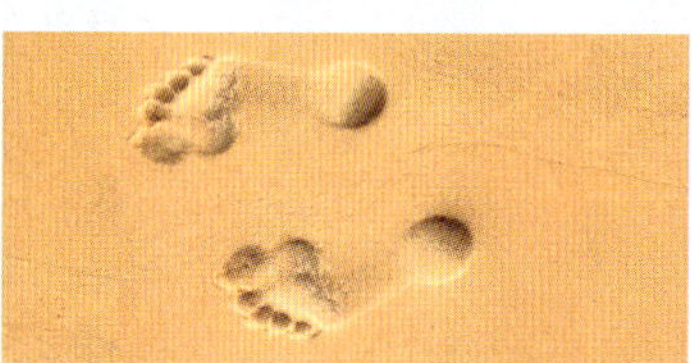

b _ _ _ _ _ _ _ _ _ _ _ _

c _ _ _ _ _ _ _ _ _

d _ _ _ _ _ _ _ _ _

e _ _ _

f _ _ _ _

2 Complete the sentences with the words from Activity 1.

a These scientists are working together in a new ....lab.......... .

b Oil, wood, and gas are different kinds of ....

c When you ride your bicycle on the road, please use the ....

d My dad is good at all winter sports, and this year he's going to teach me how to ....

e Look at the .... on the ground – big animals must live in this forest.

f Lots of different .... live on and inside each person's body.

3 Replace the underlined words with the correct words from the box.

carbon neutral	offset	second-hand	sustainable	~~store~~

a We have to <u>put</u> this food in a plastic box. ....store..........

b My sister always wears clothes that are <u>not new</u>. ....

c All the buildings in this new town need to be <u>good for the environment</u>. ....

d Many governments around the world want to be <u>putting no greenhouse gases into the atmosphere</u> in the future. ....

e Next year, I'm going to <u>do good things to change</u> my carbon footprint. ....

WHAT NEXT

1 Here are two organizations that are trying to help the environment. Which do you think is most interesting? Tick (✓) the box.

a ☐ **AeroFarms**

b ☐ **Wikkelhouse**

2 Find out more information about the organization and answer the questions.

a What does the organization do?

b Why is this good for our planet?

c What do you think the organization will do or make in the future?

Project A *Animals in danger*

1 Read the report about animal crossings. Which countries are in the report?

Animal crossings

Millions of animals die in traffic accidents every year. The good news is that there is an answer – a special crossing just for animals.

In Quintana Roo in South-Eastern Mexico, there is a big road in the middle of the jungle. When the Mexican government built the road, they put ten special crossings under it, so that animals can travel safely from one part of the jungle to the other. They built the crossings for jaguars – which use them at night – but eighteen other large animal species also use them.

In Canada, there is a road in the Banff National Park with thirty-eight crossings under it and six crossings over it. Different animals prefer different crossings. Grizzly bears, for example, prefer the crossings that go over the road.

There are now 90% fewer accidents on the road because of the animal crossings.

grizzly bears

An animal crossing in Banff National Park, Canada

2 Correct the factual mistakes in the notes below.

- Animal crossings can only go under a road.
- Jaguars use the crossings in Quintana Roo during the day.
- A total of eighteen large species use the Quintana Roo crossings.
- The Banff National Park is in the USA.
- Polar bears prefer crossings over the road.
- There are no traffic accidents because of the Banff crossings.

3 Choose the best ending a–c for the report.

a These animal crossings are good news for the environment, but they are only good for countries like Mexico and Canada.

b These animal crossings are good news for the environment. They show that people and animals can live together.

c These animal crossings are good news for the environment. We must stop driving cars to protect animals like jaguars and bears.

4 Order paragraphs a–d to make a report about the blue iguana.

a ☐ Scientists had to do something. They took some iguana eggs, and when the baby iguanas were born they protected them. Most iguanas now live in the Salinas Reserve which is protected land, so they are now safe.

b ☐ The changes worked. Today, there are almost 1,000 blue iguanas on Grand Cayman. Many species are becoming extinct, but this story shows that people can save wild animals that are in danger.

c ☐ The blue iguana was in danger. It only lives on the Grand Cayman island, and people were building too many houses where the iguanas lived. There were also other dangers. In the past, people brought dogs and cats to the island, and these animals were killing the iguanas.

d ☐ This report looks at the blue iguana. In 2002, there were less than twenty-five wild blue iguanas in the world. The species was nearly extinct.

blue iguana

5 Think of a good news story about an animal in danger. Write notes, and then write a report about it.

Project B *A green problem*

1 Match the reporter's questions a–g with the sailor's answers 1–7.

Questions

a What problem do you want to talk about today?

b How did you find out about it?

c What is the problem? Tell me more.

d How did it happen?

e Will it be a problem in the future?

f Is it a danger for wild animals?

g Do scientists know how to stop it?

Answers

1 The Great Pacific Garbage Patch is a very polluted place. It's a large area of sea that's full of plastic waste.

2 I saw it when I was sailing in the Pacific.

3 Yes, because the sea will become more polluted.

4 No, they don't, but they are thinking of new ideas.

5 Yes, because fish sometimes think the plastic is food, and they can die after eating it.

6 Most of the waste has come from people on land, and some of it from boats and ships.

7 I want to tell you about the Great Pacific Garbage Patch.

2 Match a–e with pictures 1–5 to learn more about the Great Pacific Garbage Patch.

a ☐ The Great Pacific Garbage Patch is in different areas, including the Eastern Garbage Patch and the Western Garbage Patch.

b ☐ Most of the waste comes from rivers on land.

c ☐ It isn't just fish who can die after eating plastic from the Great Pacific Garbage Patch.

d ☐ Charles Moore found the Great Pacific Garbage Patch in 1997, but some of the plastic waste is over fifty years old.

e ☐ Very small pieces of plastic called 'microplastics' are also in the water.

1

2

3

4

5

3 Think of or research a 'green' problem. Then write the answers to these questions, if you can.

1 What problem do you want to talk about today?

....

....

2 How did you find out about it?

....

....

3 What is the problem? Tell me more.

....

....

4 How did it happen?

....

....

5 Will it be a problem in the future?

....

....

6 Is it a danger for wild animals?

....

....

7 Do scientists know how to stop it?

....

....

Option: Imagine you're on television. Work in pairs to ask and answer the questions.

Student A: You're a reporter. Ask the questions.

Student B: Answer the questions.

Sequencing words: *at first, then, next, later, in the end, at the same time*

We use sequencing words to show the order in which things happen. Sequencing words usually come at the beginning of a sentence. We use at first for things that happen first. We use then, next, or later for things that follow. We use at the same time for things that happen at the same time, and we use in the end for things that come last.

At first, there was an earthquake. Then, the villagers saw a big wall of water. Next, a tsunami destroyed all the buildings near the sea. At the same time, everyone was trying to leave as fast as they could. Later, there was another smaller earthquake. In the end, many families lost their homes, but nobody died.

1 Put sentences a–f in order. Then complete the sentences with the sequencing words from the box.

At first	~~At the same time~~	In the end	Later	Next	Then

a [4] At the same time, boats came to take the people to hospital.

b [ ] ...., there was an explosion on *Deepwater Horizon*.

c [ ] ...., the BP oil company gave money to the people who had problems after the disaster.

d [ ] ...., there was a fire, and people were hurt.

e [ ] ...., many people had health problems, and fishermen lost their jobs.

f [ ] ...., people on the oil rig worked to stop the fire.

2 Match the sentence halves.

a At first, a Sea Shepherd ship…

b Then, the two boats…

c Next, some people from Sea Shepherd…

d Later, the captain of *Thunder*…

e In the end, *Thunder's* captain and two other men…

1 cut *Thunder's* nets.

2 asked Sea Shepherd for help because his ship was sinking.

3 began chasing the ship *Thunder* in Antarctica.

4 had to go to prison.

5 nearly crashed into each other.

How much / _How many_ + uncountable / countable nouns

We use how much and how many to ask about amounts and numbers. We use how much with uncountable nouns.

How much rain falls in the rainforests every year?

We use how many with plural countable nouns.

How many jaguars are in this national park?

3 Complete the questions with _how much_ / _how many_. Then match the questions with the answers.

a How many satellites are there in *Sentinel-1*? 6
b .... money does Greenpeace make? ....
c .... parts of the world have rainforests? ....
d .... rain do the wettest rainforests get? ....
e .... trees are cut down in the rainforests every year? ....
f .... golden toads are there in the world today? ....
g .... people were there in the world in 2020? ....
h .... penguin species are there on the Earth? ....
i .... money did the men from the ship *Thunder* have to pay? ....
j .... oil went into the sea after the *Deepwater Horizon* disaster? ....

1 Between seventeen and twenty.
2 A lot – an area as big as the country of Panama.
3 Three.
4 None – no dollars, and no pounds.
5 17 million dollars.
6 Two.
7 About 630 million litres.
8 None since 1989.
9 7.8 billion.
10 A lot of rain all year.

GRAMMAR

Articles: *a / an, the,* no article (–)

We use the indefinite article a / an when we talk about singular nouns, when it isn't clear which of several things we may mean.

A penguin can see well, both in the air and in the water.

We use a in front of a word that begins with a consonant and an in front of a word that begins with a vowel or vowel sound.

A polar bear can be two metres tall.

It's an Emperor penguin.

We use the definite article the when we talk about singular and plural nouns, when it's clear which of several things we mean.

The water in that river is polluted.

The floods here are dangerous.

We don't use an article (–) when we talk about things in general.

Penguins are very interesting animals.

Cars use fuel.

4 Complete the sentences with *a, an, the,* or –.

a Satellites like *Sentinel-1* send back .... information about our planet.

b Greenpeace is trying to protect .... trees in the world's rainforests.

c Our planet is now in .... climate emergency.

d Big areas of .... land are disappearing under water.

e Alan Rabinowitz had .... idea for a park which could protect wild animals.

f .... blue whale can be around thirty metres long.

g .... penguins that live in the Antarctic are Adélie and Emperor penguins.

h Polar bears wait on the ice to catch .... seals.

i The ship in .... longest chase at sea was called *Thunder*.

j Governments often have .... meetings about climate change.

Linkers: *and, but, because, or, so*

Linkers are words that join two sentences together to make one. We use and to link two parts of a sentence with the same idea.

Scientists got information from Sentinel-1 *and sent it to Malawi.*

We use but to link two parts of a sentence with different ideas.

Darwin travelled on the Beagle, *but he didn't get any money for his work.*

We use because to show the reason for something.

Sentinel-1 *has a lot of information about our planet because its satellites take pictures of the Earth every six days.*

We use or to give a different possibility.

Scientists have used Sentinel-1 *to get early news of earthquakes or floods.*

We use so to show the result of something.

The ice is melting, so sea levels are rising.

5 Complete the sentences with the words from the box.

and	because	because	~~but~~	but	or	so	so

a You can't see *Sentinel-1*, ...but........ it's at work twenty-four hours per day.

b Darwin was interested in plants and animals, ... he agreed to go to South America with a group of scientists.

c Finches can have strong beaks .... narrow beaks.

d These finches' beaks were different .... they ate different food.

e Trees are important .... they take carbon dioxide from the air and make oxygen.

f He visited the island, ... he didn't stay very long.

g Polar bears in the Arctic have less time for hunting, ... they are becoming thinner.

h Living a greener life means eating more vegetables .... using less energy.

Gerund as subject or object

We can use the gerund as the subject or object of a verb. To make the gerund, we usually add -ing to the verb, but when a verb ends in a consonant + -e, we remove the -e and add -ing.

Walking is better for the environment than driving. (= subject)

I'm going to stop driving. (= object)

The gerund can have its own object.

Riding a bicycle is good for the environment. *People need to stop polluting the Earth.*

6 Complete the sentences with the gerund (-ing) form of the verbs in the box. Write *S* for a gerund as a subject or *O* for a gerund as an object.

burn buy clean do eat find hunt ~~put~~ protect protest travel watch

a ...Putting... pesticides on plants affects the environment. ....S....

b In 1972, the US government stopped .... nuclear tests on the island of Amchitka. ....

c .... coal puts greenhouse gases into the atmosphere. ....

d For some animals, ... food will become harder because more and more land is disappearing under the sea. ....

e People all around the world enjoy .... food that comes from rainforest plants. ....

f John Muir loved .... to wild, beautiful places in the USA. ....

g .... animals isn't possible in a national park. ....

h .... the Great Barrier Reef is difficult because the sea water is becoming warmer. ....

i Millions of people like .... whales in the world's oceans every year. ....

j In Japan, the government hasn't finished .... the soil around the Fukushima power plant. ....

k .... second-hand clothes helps us to have a smaller carbon footprint. ....

l Greta Thunberg began .... about climate change when she was fifteen years old. ....

Forming questions: Present Simple, Past Simple, Present Continuous and Past Continuous

To form questions with the Present Simple, we use do / does + subject + infinitive without *to*.

Sentinel-1 *works all day and all night.*	*When does* Sentinel-1 *work?*
Emperor penguins live in the Antarctic.	*Where do Emperor penguins live?*

To form questions with the Past Simple, we use did + subject + infinitive without *to*.

Darwin wrote a book called On the Origin of Species.	*What did Darwin write?*

To form questions with the Present Continuous, we use am / is / are + subject + the -ing form of the verb.

The environment is changing all the time.	*What is the environment doing?*

To form questions with the Past Continuous, we use was / were + subject + the -ing form of the verb.

In 1859, everyone was talking about Darwin's book.	*What was everyone talking about in 1859?*

7 Read the questions and answers. Complete each question with the subject and the correct form of the verb in brackets.

a How often does Sentinel-1 take (*Sentinel-1* / take) pictures of our planet?
Every six days.

b Where .... (Darwin / go) on the *Beagle*?
He went to South America and the Galapagos Islands.

c Why .... (some islands / disappear)?
Because sea levels are rising.

d How .... (rainforests / affect) other parts of the world?
They take carbon dioxide from the air.

e Where .... (Alan Rabinowitz / live) when he had a plane crash?
He was living in Belize.

f What .... (polar bears / eat) during the winter?
They eat seals.

If clauses

We can use if clauses to talk about a condition – something that must happen so that another thing can happen. In this case, we use the present tense in the *if* clause and can / can't in the main clause.

If we travel by train, we can help the environment.

If the water is polluted, we can't drink it.

We can also use if clauses to talk about a future possibility. In this case, we use the present tense in the *if* clause, and will / won't in the main clause.

If we use less coal, the air will be cleaner.

If the Earth's temperature rises, it won't come down again.

8 Match the sentence halves.

a If you look into the sky,…
b If plastic goes into the sea,…
c If we don't stop burning fuel,…
d If an Emperor penguin dives,…
e If you live in a sustainable house,…

1 you won't make a lot of waste.
2 it can hurt the animals that live there.
3 it can stay under the water for twenty minutes.
4 you won't see *Sentinel-1*.
5 there will be more greenhouse gases.

9 Complete the sentences with *can, can't, will* or *won't*.

a If scientists have information about the Earth from satellites, they ...can... use it to help people who are in danger.
b If farmers use pesticides, the insects on their plants .... die.
c If more land disappears under the sea, some migrating birds .... find places to rest.
d If there is only a small number of animals of the same species, that species .... easily disappear.
e If you put wild animals in a national park, those animals .... be protected.
f If a car doesn't have fuel inside it, you .... drive it.
g If food grows in radioactive soil, it .... be safe to eat.
h If everyone uses less energy, it .... be good for our planet.

DOMINOES Your Choice

Read *Dominoes* for pleasure, or to develop language skills. It's your choice.

Each *Dominoes* reader includes:
- a good story to enjoy
- integrated activities to develop reading skills and increase vocabulary
- task-based projects – perfect for CEFR portfolios
- contextualized grammar activities.

Each *Dominoes* pack contains a reader and an excitingly dramatized audio recording of the story

If you liked this *Domino*, read these:

White Fang

Jack London

Life is hard and dangerous for both people and animals in the frozen Canadian North. For a wolf like White Fang it is a continuous fight to find food – a fight in which many animals die.

When White Fang meets the people of the North – first Indians and then White Men – he learns to live with them like a dog. But some men are cruel to their dogs and others are kind. Will White Fang's life be any easier now?

Jemma's Jungle Adventure

Anne Collins

Jemma is very excited when she joins an expedition to the island of Kamora. She hopes to learn about doing scientific research, and to find a very rare bird of paradise.

She is happy to meet the famous Dr Malone and the wise Dr Al Barwani, and to help to research birds, snakes, and insects. But things start to go wrong. Someone has a terrible secret, and there is danger for Jemma – and for the bird.

Who has a secret plan, and what is it? What will happen to the bird? And what will happen to Jemma?

	CEFR	Cambridge Exams	IELTS	TOEFL iBT	TOEIC
Level 3	B1	PET	4.0	57-86	550
Level 2	A2–B1	KET-PET	3.0-4.0	–	390
Level 1	A1–A2	YLE Flyers/KET	3.0	–	225
Starter & Quick Starter	A1	YLE Movers	1.0–2.0	–	–

You can find details and a full list of books and teachers' resources on our website:
www.oup.com/elt/gradedreaders